Real World
Colouring Book
For Advanced Users & Adults

Copyright 2019 By John Boom

50 Images

Created From Real Life Photos
For You To Colour As You Please.

ISBN 978-0-359-79168-2

9 780359 791682

90000